Mastering The Mental Side Of Football

HK

Hemispheric Kinesiology

Ernest Solivan

ISBN: 978-0-6151-7357-3

"I've found that prayers work best when you have big players."

> *Knute Rockne*
> *Notre Dame*

Table of Contents

Table of Contents

Introduction

With the advent of quantum physics, science must now acknowledge that there are things that happen below our level of conscious awareness that dramatically affect the experiences we create. The HK Football program is designed to work on a quantum level, or below your level of conscious awareness. That is where the blockages are preventing you from reaching your full potential to become a better player.

This is a book about Hemispheric Kinesiology (HK) and how you can use it to achieve peak performance as a football player. HK is a success technology that provides you with a perspective that allows you to objectively look at the experiences you are creating on the field as well as in your personal life, and through that objectivity create positive change that will improve your athletic performance so that you play your best during competition.

The first part of the book explains the development of HK and provides a foundational context on how your mind and brain influence the experiences (both positive and negative) you create on and off the field. The second part explains how to use HK to become a premier player at your position.

 HK's most salient characteristic is that it offers a very credible, rational and viable explanation as to why you experience performance problems during competition and offers a remedy that will allow you minimize and/or eliminate those uncharacteristic mental errors during competition so that you may play to the best of your ability.

There is an old saying that you cannot teach an old dog new tricks. This is a testament to how difficult change is for just about everyone. There are basically three elements necessary to create change in your life. They are Sensation, Perception and Conception. Sensation is the capacity to experience; Perception is the capacity to be aware of what you are experiencing; and Conception is taking action to begin the process of change, or it can also represent a rebirthing into some new experience.

I refer to HK as a language of change because it embodies all the elements necessary to facilitate and accelerate positive change in the athletes who experience it. HK does not diagnosis or label. Please respect the context in which I present this extraordinary and very effective discipline. It works on the simple premise that if it stresses you to play football, you are not going to do it well.

Please set aside your prejudices, beliefs and judgments and do your best to keep an open mind. HK is a little different twist on psychology. This discipline was created with the intention of allowing you to help yourself facilitate and accelerate positive changes that will immeasurably improve the quality of your life on the football field, as well as in your personal life. And, isn't that what we are all looking for?

It is said that football is 95% mental and 5% physical. When you have finished reading *Mastering The Mental Side Of Football* you will understand why football is 100% mental.

The Mind

When you set a goal to do something one of two things will happen. You will either succeed or fail. What determines your success or failure is the information contained in your Mind. This stored information is the information you will use while attempting to accomplish your goal.

If the information in your Mind supports you in successfully completing your goal, the accomplishment of your goal will be easy and almost effortless. However, if the information in your Mind does not support you in successfully accomplishing your goal, the accomplishment of your goal will be very difficult and require a tremendous amount of effort.

The Mind is generally thought to be the seat of consciousness. It is made up of every aspect of our being. There are many philosophies that view the Mind in a way that has created numerous fragments, i.e., the spiritual mind, the emotional mind, the etheric mind, etc. I found all these subdivisions to be very confusing.

In HK I rely upon the very old axiomatic metaphysical concept known as "cause and effect." Several of the theories that support cause and effect are, "for every action there is an opposite and equal reaction;" "water seeks it own level" and "what goes around comes around." In HK, I start by focusing on the desired effect, and work backwards to the cause.

Although I cannot see a football player's Mind, I can see the experiences that Mind is creating. For instance, if I am working with a player who cannot make the roster of an NFL team after the final preseason game, I must assume that he has information stored in his Mind to support him in doing that or he would be doing something else.

It is important to note that your Mind supports you in everything you do. If you are failing, your Mind is supporting you in failing and it is doing so based upon information it has stored in its memory banks relating to success and failure. The football player's body is merely acting out (i.e., failing to make the roster) based upon this stored information, and it does it automatically.

To fully understand cause and effect, you must first understand that before anything physical happens in our lives, it must first start as a thought. So, if you want to change your undesirable experiences, you must change the thoughts that are responsible for creating those undesirable experiences.

For example, the information stored in the football player's Mind is the cause while the experience he is creating (failing to make the roster), or the acting out of his physical body, is the effect. The effect that this football player is creating in his reality is clearly an undesirable effect, and he will continue to create this experience until something changes.

The information he is accessing is not supporting him in succeeding. The goal of HK is to change the information in this player's Mind, and to do it as quickly as possible. Once he accomplishes that, his experience will change. When you change your thinking, you will change the experiences you are creating with those thoughts.

Before I explain how this is accomplished, it is important to establish a context and foundation whereby all the contributing factors to this failure phenomenon may be examined and understood. It is noteworthy to point out that in HK, all we are dealing with is information. For instance, although an emotion is something we can feel, it is stored in the Mind as information.

The Mind has two parts. The Conscious Mind and the Subconscious Mind.

The Conscious Mind

The Conscious Mind is known as the "knower" because it has the ability to be aware of itself. It has the capacity to be aware of what it is thinking and feeling in the normal waking state. It also has the ability to know what it is doing and why. One of the major functions of the Conscious Mind is its use of volition. Volition is defined as, "the act of using the will; exercise of the will as in deciding what to do; a conscious or deliberate decision of choices thus made."

You are where you are in your life right now as a direct result of the choices you have made using the volitional part of your Conscious Mind. The Conscious Mind provides us with short-term memory and can only focus on one thing at a time. The Conscious Mind uses the five senses; sight, hearing, smell, taste and touch, to collect information which allows it to experience awareness.

The Conscious Mind uses this collected information to formulate your self-image, your prejudices, and your belief system. The most important function of the Conscious Mind is that it allows us to set goals. The information collected by the Conscious Mind will influence the formulation and successful completion of the goals we set throughout our lives.

So, what happens when the Conscious Mind, using its volition, decides to engage in some particular activity like football? Well, it types out a memo of the instructions and sends it to the Subconscious Mind.

The Subconscious Mind

When you engage in a particular activity, like football, it is the responsibility of your Conscious Mind to decide the nature of the activity. Your Conscious Mind will send instructions to your Subconscious Mind, "Send me all the information you have relating to football."

If the information accessed from your Subconscious Mind is supportive, you will perform the activity easily and efficiently. However, if the information accessed from your Subconscious Mind is not supportive or contradicts the goal set by your Conscious Mind, your activity will become very difficult and require a tremendous amount of effort.

The Subconscious Mind is a part of the Mind known as the "doer" because it merely does what it is programmed to do. Unlike the Conscious Mind, the Subconscious Mind does not have the capacity to exercise volition, it merely "does."

The Subconscious Mind acts out thorough the physical body and uses information it has stored in its memory banks relating to football. This "acting out" is done instantaneously and automatically. The information arrived into the Subconscious Mind through the Conscious Mind using the five senses (sight, hearing, smell, taste, and touch).

The Subconscious Mind is a storage facility for all information that enters through the Conscious Mind. The one important feature to note about the Subconscious Mind is that when it is storing information it is impersonal. It doesn't say, "I am not going to store this experience because it was a bad experience." IT STORES EVERYTHING! The Subconscious Mind also provides us with long-term memory, and is the receptacle for our belief system.

The Subconscious Mind does not have a sense of humor. It cannot distinguish between a joke and something serious. Additionally, the Subconscious Mind cannot distinguish between something real or imagined.

The Subconscious Mind can be likened to the hard drive of your computer with one notable exception. When using a computer, you have the option of saving or erasing the information on your screen. Every piece of information that enters the Subconscious Mind is stored for future use.

Your Conscious Mind will eventually use this subconsciously stored information when it engages in an activity that corresponds to the information in storage. The Subconscious Mind will provide the Conscious Mind with whatever information is has available. The information can be supportive as well as non-supportive information.

If there is one thing I would like you to get from reading this book it's that everything we do is subconscious. Do you remember years ago as a child when you were first learning to tie your shoes? At first it took a tremendous amount of concentration and effort. Now, you do it without thinking because it has now become a subconscious act.

That is exactly what is happening with every other aspect of your life. When you are on the field and the ball is snapped you don't stop and ask yourself "What do I do now?" Everything is moving to quickly for your Conscious Mind to get involved and you are at the mercy of the information stored in your Subconscious Mind and it will dramatically influence how you perform that day. That is, your physical body will "act out" based on whatever information is stored in your Subconscious Mind.

There is a very integral component of the Mind that gets involved when the Conscious and the Subconscious Mind interact. It is known to as the Critical Factor.

The Critical Factor

After information enters the Conscious Mind, it is reviewed prior to storage in the Subconscious Mind. The responsibility for this task belongs to a component of the Mind known as the Critical Factor. The Critical Factor literally criticizes or reviews information that comes into conscious awareness. After its review, the Critical Factor must make a decision regarding the disposition of the information. The Critical Factor has two options. It can either store the information, or reject it.

Everyone knows that the color of the sky is blue, but suppose I told you that the color of the sky was red. When that statement enters your Conscious Mind, your Critical Factor will stop it momentarily and say something to the effect, "Let me check the information I have in subconscious storage relating to the color of the sky."

The Critical Factor checks and discovers that the information stored in the Subconscious Mind indicates that the color of the sky is blue. The Critical Factor proceeds to reject the statement, "The sky is red."

Getting back to the player who could not make the final preseason cut we must assume that the experience he created responded by corresponding to the information stored in his Subconscious Mind. It's as if his Subconscious Mind goes on "red alert" and proceeds to sabotage his success using his physical body.

It is absolutely crucial that you understand the role your Critical Factor plays in sabotaging your athletic performances. It is not being vindictive, but rather impersonal. It is basically saying, "I would love to support you in becoming all pro this season, but I just don't have the information stored to support you in doing that." When you change the information, you change the experience.

If you are a college player, it's your critical factor that is stopping you from being drafted by an NFL team. If you are an NFL defensive lineman, it is your critical factor that is stopping you from recording any sacks during the year.

Imagine the Critical Factor as a guard, and that it is guarding all information coming into and leaving the Mind. How do you change this information? How do you change subconsciously stored information causing you to exhibit undesirable behavior patterns, or causing you to athletically perform well below your true potential? In order to change subconsciously stored information, we must achieve Critical Factor Bypass.

Critical Factor Bypass

Critical Factor Bypass occurs when new information is allowed to bypass the Critical Factor of the Mind in an effort to change old information stored in the Subconscious Mind. HK can achieve Critical Factor Bypass, which enables you to literally change subconsciously stored information preventing you from playing your best during competition.

Using HK to achieve Critical Factor Bypass allows us to accelerate change for the athletes who experience it. In order to more fully understand Critical Factor Bypass, we must first look to the advertising industry.

On many occasions advertising agencies will send sales copy to a psychologist and ask, "Will this copy achieve Critical Factor Bypass for our product?" The ad agencies know that if they can achieve Critical Factor Bypass on anyone who hears or sees their commercials, their chances of selling their product or service are greatly enhanced. They carefully choose the people who star in these commercials, carefully choose the wording, and carefully choose the scenarios.

How can they motivate someone to buy their product or service? One way to do it is using fear in the form of authority figures. It cannot be done blatantly. It must be subtle. Have you ever noticed that in many commercials, ad agencies will use policemen, judges, doctors, or firemen. All these professions represent authority figures and the ad agencies know that when a policeman tells you to do something, you normally do it without question. You do what you are told because the policeman was able to achieve Critical Factor Bypass.

Another very subtle tactic ad agencies will use to create Critical Factor Bypass is race and gender. I once saw a print ad that contained a Caucasian, an African-American, an Asian, an older gentleman, an older woman, a young man, and a young woman. They covered a lot of bases with that ad and they did it subjectively (subconsciously).

Sometimes the ad agencies will appeal to your emotions. I am certain you have seen the Michelin Tire commercial with a baby sitting in a tire. That commercial has been running for years. This particular commercial has been successful because the ad agency was able to achieve Critical Factor Bypass by using the baby to appeal to the emotions of the viewer.

Michelin must be selling a lot of tires, or they would not continue to use this very effective commercial. Some of the other tactics used by ad agencies are humor and money. In fact, the next time you view or hear a commercial advertisement ask yourself, "What are they doing in this commercial to achieve Critical Factor Bypass to motivate me to purchase their product or service?"

In order for that college player to get drafted by an NFL team, and the defensive lineman who cannot record a sack to change their fortunes, they must bypass their Critical Factors and change the subconsciously stored information preventing them from getting what they want.

.

I will explain in a later chapter how we are able to achieve Critical Factor Bypass using HK. For now, we have examined the nuances of the Mind to include the Conscious Mind, the Subconscious Mind, the Critical Factor, and Critical Factor Bypass. Your Mind must act out through your physical body and it does this using your Brain.

The Brain

Although the Mind is the decision maker, it is the brain's responsibility to carry out those instructions. The brain is a part of the Central Nervous System composed of approximately 10 billion nerve cells.

Each cell is linked to one another, and together they are responsible for the control of all functions in the physical body. The brain disseminates these instructions throughout the physical body using information provided by the Mind in the form of electrical impulses.

As I had mentioned earlier, working with the Mind is so challenging because we cannot see it. Although we cannot see a player's Mind, we can ascertain facts by observing what kinds of experiences that player's Mind is creating.

If, for example, one of your teammates is struggling at his position, I have to assume that there is information stored in his Mind to support him in struggling, or he would be doing something else.

`The brain is an organ consisting of three major components. The Left Hemisphere, The Right Hemisphere and the Corpus Callosum. Although these three components are integral, they each have very specific and different functions, and can function independently should the need arise. The Left Hemisphere of the brain controls the right side of the physical body, while the Right Hemisphere controls the left side.

We need only look at a stroke victim to understand this phenomenon. Notice that in the majority of the cases only one side of the body is paralyzed. That's because the hemisphere of the brain on the opposite side of the affected area was so severely damaged during the stroke that it manifested as paralysis.

The corresponding side of the physical body is not receiving electrical impulses (information) from the damaged hemisphere resulting in partial or total paralysis. There are degrees of dysfunction between the brain and the physical body, and total paralysis represents the extreme during a stroke.

Since the Left and Right Hemispheres of the brain can function independently and have their own responsibilities, they need some way to communicate. This is accomplished using the Corpus Callosum.

The Corpus Callosum is a band of nerve fibers that connect the Left and Right Hemispheres of the brain. The hemispheres share and exchange information (electrical impulses) that will eventually be disseminated to the physical body.

I realized in my research in working with athletes over the years that the hemispheres of the brain have a tendency to "weaken" or "switch off." When one hemisphere is switched off, the opposite hemisphere will dominate. For instance, if a your Left Hemisphere is switched off, your Right Hemisphere will dominate whatever activity you may be involved in, and vice versa. The hemispheres of the brain are continually influenced by and are reacting to, stimuli in your immediate external environment.

An excellent case in point occurred when I had worked with the Arizona State University men's golf team in 1991. The director of the golf program was observing one of the sessions with one of the team members on the driving range. He commented that the player was muscle testing weak for everything, as all the statements were relating to golf.

So I turned to the young man and asked him what his favorite school subject was. "Math," he replied. I then asked him to imagine himself doing Math. The young man muscle tested strong, and both hemispheres of his brain were strong or switched on.

Then I asked him to imagine himself playing in a school golf tournament. The young man muscle tested weak, and both hemispheres of his brain were weak or switched off.

When he was doing Math, his physical body was relaxed, and both hemispheres of his brain were strong or switched on. The information he was accessing from his Subconscious Mind relating to Math supported him in doing it well and he excelled.

However, when he stepped on the golf course, it immediately created stress in his physical body, which weakened or switched off both hemispheres of his brain. Whatever he did on the golf course was a struggle.

The brain does basically three things. It processes (learns), stores, and disseminates information. What kind of information? That would be any and all information relating to pictures, sounds, fragrances, culinary data, and touch. All three of the major components of the brain come into play when the brain is exercising these functions. Let's first examine the Left Hemisphere of the brain.

The Left Hemisphere

When the Left Hemisphere of the brain processes (learns) information, it only understands words, language and numbers. That's because the Left Hemisphere processes information sequentially, or one piece at a time. The Left Hemisphere is one-dimensional, and can only focus on one thing at a time.

The Left Hemisphere controls the right side of the physical body and it accomplishes this by sending information in the form of electrical impulses.

When the Left Hemisphere of the brain weakens or switches off, during the processing or learning stage, it's as if a biological short circuit occurs in the electrical field in the physical body, and the incoming information never reaches the hemisphere of the brain that is switched off.

Incoming information will only store in the hemisphere that is switched on. For instance, if your Right Hemisphere is switched off while your brain is learning, the incoming information will store in your Left Hemisphere.

Now, because there was no information stored in your Right Hemisphere, when it's time for your brain to disseminate the information to you at some point in the future, you will only receive information from your Left Hemisphere. It's as if you are only getting half the information.

When the Left Hemisphere of the brain stores information, it will only store sequential information such as words, language and numbers. It will store information that is logical and organized. In other words, the information stored in the Left Hemisphere must be structured.

When the brain disseminates information to the physical body, the Left and Right Hemispheres deal with different and specific information. The Left Hemisphere of the brain provides the physical body with the following information and attributes:

Logic, action, decision making, critical, one-dimensional, mechanical, compulsive, doubt, cautious, judgmental, hard working, limitation, shame, rational, stoic, organization, reasoning, specificity, structure, boundaries, rules, rigidity, opinionated, intense, impersonal, cold, unfeeling, introverted, controlled, predictable, restricted, precise, serious, conservative, quiet, hard, intolerant, auditory, scientific, temporal (the now), arrogant, fearful and finite.

When you engage in an activity and the Right Hemisphere of your brain is weak or switched off, your physical body is only receiving information, or a majority of the information, from your Left Hemisphere. This causes you to become left-brain dominant while you are engaged in that particular activity. The result is you will exhibit one or more of the personality traits listed above.

For example, a left-brain dominant individual is very introverted, dresses very conservatively, and are very critical of others. If you ever encounter an overly critical individual please know that the person he is most critical of is himself. By criticizing others he is attempting to direct all attention to someone else so that no one can see his shortcomings.

This abnormal brain dominance creates conditions of extremes. When we access information from only one hemisphere of the brain, it's as if we are only receiving half the information available to us. This phenomenon can create very dysfunctional experiences for the left-brain dominate individual.

Since our thoughts create our experiences, you can clearly see that many of us are using only half the information available to us. Where is the other half of this information located? It is located in the Right Hemisphere of the brain.

The Right Hemisphere

When the Right Hemisphere of the brain processes information, it only understands movement and pictures. That's because the Right Hemisphere is spatial and can process information collectively rather than sequentially. This collectiveness allows it to process large amounts of information at one time. It will process information that has no structure.

For instance, if you were looking at a picture of a landscape with your Left Hemisphere, you would have to look at every piece of the picture individually because the Left Hemisphere processes information sequentially. You cannot see the whole picture if you are only looking at one piece.

The collective capabilities of the Right Hemisphere allows you to see the whole picture, while the Left Hemisphere provides you with the capacity to structure the collective information in the form of discernible images.

When we examine this phenomenon during the learning stage of our development, we can clearly see how the hemispheres of the brain influence how we learn. Let's look at an elementary school student named Harold. He is learning to read the sentence, "See Jack jump." If Harold had the Right Hemisphere of his brain weak or switched off while reading this sentence, his Left Hemisphere would dominate.

Now, keeping in mind that the Left Hemisphere processes information sequentially, Harold's Left Hemisphere will know and understand the words <u>see</u>, <u>Jack</u>, and <u>jump</u> individually. However, because Harold's Right Hemisphere is weak or switched off, he will have difficulty achieving total comprehension. His ability to conceptualize becomes severely compromised.

In order for that to happen, Harold would have to send the information from his Left Hemisphere, via the corpus callosum, to the Right Hemisphere, and request additional information such as a visual of a boy jumping. With both hemispheres of his brain participating in the learning process, Harold will achieve total comprehension, no matter what he is learning.

When the brain disseminates information to the physical body, the Right and Left Hemispheres deal with different and specific information. The Right Hemisphere of the brain provides the physical body with the following information and attributes:

Feelings, emotions, relaxation, beliefs, creativity, flexibility, physical movement, tolerance, visualization, artistic, spatial, self-esteem, forgiveness, unstructured, generalizations, procrastination, compassion, optimism, passive, funny, unreasonable, loud, expressive, foolish, passion, charming, humility, love, intuition, uncontrollable, multidimensional, imagination, addictions, laid back, open-minded, unorganized and infinite.

When the Left Hemisphere of your brain is weak or switched off, the Right Hemisphere will dominate your activities, from your decision making to your personality. Since your physical body is only receiving information from the Right Hemisphere of your brain, you will exhibit one or more of the above listed personality traits and attributes.

Think of the many times you had been saddened by an experience in your life, or the many times you have been very passionate about a particular cause? It is during these times when the Right Hemisphere of your brain was dominating your thinking.

The objective in HK is to switch on both hemispheres of your brain in relationship to a thought, statement or action. Having both hemispheres of your brain switched on insures that you will have access to information such as judgment, analysis and structure (Left Hemisphere), as well as creativity, imagination and intuition (Right Hemisphere).

With both hemispheres of your brain providing your physical body with information, you will experience total balance in your life, no matter what the activity.

A great analogy for explaining hemispheric balance is water. The Right Hemisphere can be likened to boiling hot water, while the Left

Hemisphere is ice-cold water. By themselves, their temperatures are very uncomfortable. However, when you mix them together, you get a warm, comfortable and balanced temperature. When both hemispheres of your brain are switched on, you enter a mental space that athletes refer to as "The Zone."

Another salient difference between the hemispheres worthy of note is that the Left Hemisphere deals with "old" information, while the Right Hemisphere deals with "new" information. I once worked with a player who wanted to successfully try out for his high school team. When I muscle tested him for the goal he had his right hemisphere weak or switched off, while his left hemisphere was strong or switched on.

This told me that he was approaching his goal with his left hemisphere and that he was using "old" information. In other words, he was saying, "What did I do last week to make the high school team, what did I do the week before to make the team?" Without the creativity provided by the right hemisphere in the form of "new" information, his goal will be a struggle.

This may explain why some people seem to make the same mistakes over and over, or repeat the same behavior patterns throughout their lives in spite of their efforts to change. When you are in your Left Hemisphere, you will continue to use old information even though it didn't work last week or last month.

Without the new information provided by the Right Hemisphere in the form of creativity, it's as if you are walking through a mental revolving door and you keep creating the same awful experience over and over. This new information augments and integrates with the old information allowing you to constructively handle whatever challenges you may be encountering at that moment.

There is another excellent analogy to contrast the hemispheres of the brain, and how they handle specific tasks. Let's assume that you have just purchased something that requires assembly.

The Left Hemisphere of your brain will approach the task by saying something like, "Where are the instructions to this thing (?); I can't put this together without the directions!" Remember that because the Left Hemisphere is using old information, it is basically asking, "Show me the way some else did it, then I can do it."

Conversely, the Right Hemisphere will approach that same task by saying, "Hey, even if we don't have the instructions, let's put it together anyway." That's because the Right Hemisphere is providing the physical body with new information in the form of creativity, and will figure it out eventually. The Right Hemisphere will risk (no instructions), while the Left Hemisphere will tend to play it safe (must have instructions).

If your left hemisphere is dominating your thinking during a game as a defensive back for instance, you will have a tendency to play it safe and stay back and give the receiver the short stuff. If your right hemisphere is dominating your thinking you will try for the interception and risk the receiver catching the pass for a long gain.

When you can function on the football field with both hemispheres of your brain strong or switched on, you will achieve a level of play that most players just dream of. With access to structure, judgment and organization (Left Hemisphere), and creativity, intuition and imagination (Right Hemisphere), every decision you make supports you in being in the right place at the right time and just allows you to play your best.

In HK it is imperative that we know what activity is taking place in the physical body in relationship to a statement, thought or action. This is accomplished using Muscle Testing.

Muscle Testing

There are three vital pieces of information necessary in HK in relationship to the subject matter that muscle testing allows me to obtain in relationship to a statement, thought or action. First, muscle testing allows me to determine whether the physical body is weak or strong. Secondly, muscle testing allows me to determine the condition of the hemispheres of the brain. Thirdly, muscle testing allows me to post test and validate that the stress has been cleared from the physical body.

Muscle testing is a technique that has been widely used in the alternative health field for years and has been used in a variety of applications. I use muscle testing to determine whether stress is present in the physical body relating to a statement, thought or action.

Since the physical body is merely acting out based upon information contained in your Subconscious Mind, muscle testing allows me to tap into that subconsciously stored information.

In his book "Switching On," Dr. Paul Dennison defines muscle testing as:

"Muscle testing is the art of isolating and testing one muscle at a time in order to determine if it is 'weak' or 'strong', relative to the strength of the individual being tested."

There are forty-two muscle groups in the physical body. In HK, I muscle test the deltoid muscle. The deltoid is the larger triangular muscle of the shoulder, which raises the arm away from the side. If you held your right arm straight out from your side, parallel to the ground, and lifted your arm upward from that point, it is the deltoid muscle that allows you to execute that movement.

When I muscle test a player I will ask him to:

1. Stand with weight evenly distributed on both feet;
2. I have the player hold his left or right arm straight out or parallel to the ground;
3. I face the player standing in front of the outstretched arm;
4. I ask the player to look straight ahead and extend the fingers of his outstretched arm so that they are parallel to the ground;
5. I place my left hand on the player's left shoulder for support;
6. I place my right hand, using only two fingers (index and middle fingers) on top of the player's outstretched arm between the elbow and wrist;
7. The player is now ready to be muscle tested;
8. I will ask the player to resist upwards slightly, towards the sky, while I apply about 2 ounces of pressure downward towards the ground. This allows both the player and myself to get a feel for the muscle test.

The key to muscle testing effectively is 2-2-2. Use two fingers, apply two ounces of pressure, and hold for two seconds. There are two possible responses to a muscle test. Strong or weak.

A strong muscle test indicates that my downward pressing motion was unable to budge the player's arm. A strong muscle test also indicates that there was no stress present in the player's physical body relating the statement, thought or action for which I muscle tested.

A weak muscle test indicates that the player was unable to resist my downward pressure, and could not hold his arm parallel to the ground. A weak muscle test is evidence that stress was present in the player's physical body relating to the statement, thought or action for which we muscle tested.

What does a strong vs a weak muscle test tell me, if anything? Well, if I had had a running back make the statement, "My goal is to gain more than 100 yards per game, every game," the strong muscle test signifies that the player's physical body would totally support him in successfully accomplishing his goal.

The absence of stress in the player's physical body indicates that there is information stored in his Subconscious Mind that would support him in accomplishing his goal.

On the other hand, had the player muscle tested weak to the statement relating to rushing for 100 yards per game, the weak muscle test indicates the presence of stress in the player's physical body relating to the statement.

It basically stressed the subject to say, "My goal is to gain more than 100 yard per game, every game." The weak muscle test tells me that the information stored in the player's Subconscious Mind will not support him in successfully accomplishing his goal.

A weak muscle test is the physical body's way of saying, "I am not doing that because I do not have information stored in my memory banks to support you, or that the information I have stored contradicts whatever it is you want to do."

The second piece of information I can obtain using muscle testing is the condition of the Right or Left Hemispheres of the brain in relationship to a statement, thought or action. For instance, when checking the condition of the Left Hemisphere, I merely touch the left side of the player's head and muscle test.

If I record a strong muscle test, the hemisphere is switched on. If I record a weak muscle test, the Left Hemisphere is switched off. I would do likewise to check the condition of the Right Hemisphere.

Checking the hemispheres of the brain allows me to determine how the subject would function while engaged in the activity for which we are muscle testing. For example, if the running back had had his Left Hemisphere switched on and his Right Hemisphere switched off, his Left Hemisphere would dominate his approach to the goal.

He would exhibit the personality traits and attributes listed under the Left Hemisphere of the brain. The successful accomplishment of his goal will be a struggle because he would be lacking information such as intuition, creativity and imagination. Information provided by the Right Hemisphere of the brain.

Thirdly, and most importantly, muscle testing allows me to validate, through post testing, that the stress relating to the subject matter has been cleared from the player's physical body. If I have you say "I am an all pro player," and you muscle test weak, and then have you say it again, and you muscle test strong, something obviously changed in your physical body and the way it reacted to the statement.

In HK, muscle testing allows me access to the player's Subconscious Mind. If subconsciously stored information is to be changed, it must be done subconsciously. Muscle testing allows me to inferentially (indirectly) access information from the player's Subconscious Mind using his physical body. That's because the Mind and the physical body are integral and mirror each other. What affects the Mind affects the physical body.

When the physical body is in a weakened state, it is engaged in a phenomenon known as "sabotage." Muscle testing allows me to interpret the language used by the physical body to communicate this sabotage state, and that language is Stress.

Stress

WHENEVER THERE IS CONFLICT BETWEEN THE CONSCIOUS MIND AND THE SUBCONCIOUS MIND, THAT CONFLICT WILL ALWAYS MANIFEST IN THE PHYSICAL BODY AS STRESS!

It's as if the Conscious Mind and the Subconscious Mind are not on the same page. When stress is present in the physical body, it will always result in a weak muscle test, and cause one or both hemispheres of the brain to weaken or switch off. The presence of stress creates a short circuit in the electrical system of the physical body and causes a biological fuse to blow.

It is crucial that you understand this phenomenon because it is at this juncture in the failure process that the physical body begins to sabotage your activity. When the physical body is in this stressed state, it goes on red alert because the information in the Conscious Mind does not match the information accessed from the Subconscious Mind. The Subconscious Mind acting out through the physical body will do everything in its power to sabotage your success.

Taber's Cyclopedic Medical Dictionary defines stress as, "...the result produced when a structure, system or organism is acted upon by forces that disrupt equilibrium or produce strain...the term denotes the physical and psychological forces that are experienced by individuals." Stress has an absolutely pervasive effect on the physical body, and the prolonged presence of stress in the body can manifest pathologically (disease).

When stress is present in the physical body, it creates a myriad of physiological changes. Some of the more salient physical reactions to stress are:

* Increase in the rate and force of heart beat;
* A rise in systolic blood pressure;
* Sweating of the palms and hands;
* Dilation of the pupils;
* Decreased digestion;
* Blood distribution from less to more active organs;
* Increased blood glucose (hyperglycemia);
* Etc.

Imagine a quarterback facing 3rd and goal, down by 7 points, with time running out and all this activity is going on in his body. When stress is present in the physical body, it interrupts the electrical signals from the brain to the muscles causing the body to weaken. It is when the body is in this weakened state that the sabotaging phenomenon occurs. Our quarterback will either throw an interception or get sacked for a loss on the play.

It is when the body is in this weakened state that a defensive back will miss his assignment and leave a wide receiver wide open in the end zone. You will say and do the wrong thing, or be in the wrong place at the wrong time. This sabotaging phenomenon is so subtle that you will be totally unaware that you are doing it because it is all happening subjectively or subconsciously. That is to say, it is happening below your level of conscious awareness.

It is important to note that there are different levels and degrees of stress that may manifest in the physical body ranging from very subtle to very severe. When a quarterback throws an interception it is impossible to see stress in his body with the naked eye.

However, since his Subconscious Mind stored that information, I can access that information later by merely asking him to remember the interception he threw during the 3rd quarter on his opponent's 20 yard line and muscle test.

Please remember that it is not what you are doing, but where you are doing it. Here's why. Take a 12" wide plank and connect it to two buildings 5 feet off the ground and ask someone to walk across it. No problem. Now, take that same 12" wide plank up to the 30th floor and ask that same person to walk across it. I guarantee you will get a different response. It is not what you are doing, but where you are doing it.

What causes stress to manifest in the physical body besides walking on a 12" wide plank 30 stories high? Well, there is something that occurs while the Subconscious Mind is storing information, and it is responsible for causing stress in the physical body. This phenomenon creates what I refer to as Synthesizing Events.

Synthesizing Events

What we have learned up to this point is that the presence of stress in the physical body adversely affects us both physically and mentally. Physically, by weakening or switching off one or both sides of the physical body; and mentally, by weakening or switching off one or both hemispheres of the brain. When stress is present in the physical body, something is motivating the body to manifest stress. That something is a "synthesizing event."

A synthesizing event is created when the emotions from a traumatic experience actually synthesizes (comes together) with the information as it is being stored in the Subconscious Mind. This synthesized information remains stored and dormant in the Subconscious Mind until the Conscious Mind engages in some activity relative to the information. Once the Conscious Mind accesses this synthesized information, it will manifest in the physical body as stress.

One of the best analogies I have ever heard in describing synthesizing events is to imagine that you have just purchased a brand new boat. The hull of this boat is clean and spotless. As time passes, barnacles will attach to the hull. The more barnacles that attach to the hull, the slower the boat will travel, until the boat accumulates so many barnacles it stops all together.

Synthesizing events are like barnacles that have attached themselves to the hulls of our lives. If you accumulate enough barnacles they may manifest physically as a nervous breakdown or chronic illness, or mentally as sabotaging everything you do.

The barnacle analogy is likened to synthesizing events that players carry around with them from game to game. When you accumulate too many synthesizing events, the bottom falls out. What's responsible for creating synthesizing events? Trauma!

Webster's defines trauma as, "1. A bodily injury or shock; 2. An emotional shock, often having lasting psychic effects." As you can clearly see, trauma can be experienced both physically and mentally, and can range from mild to severe.

The physical trauma from an automobile accident, for example, will heal with time. However, the mental (emotional) trauma may stay in the physical body for years unless you take some action to clear and release it. The intention of HK is to help individuals release trauma in the form of synthesizing events from their minds manifesting as stress in their physical bodies.

The emotional trauma of the quarterback throwing an interception with 3rd and goal, or a cornerback leaving a receiver wide open in the end zone may stay with these players for an indefinite period of time

There are two types of synthesizing events. The "initial synthesizing event," and the "subsequent synthesizing event." The following analogy explains. Suppose you had a fear of heights. There was a first time you experienced that fear and it is referred to as the initial synthesizing event because it was the first time the synthesizing dynamics came into play relating to the subject matter.

That synthesized information is stored in your Subconscious Mind, and will remain dormant until you go near a high place again. Once this happens, the Conscious Mind sends instructions to the Subconscious Mind, "Send me all the information you have stored relating to being near a high place."

The stored information from the first experience comes up, and since an emotion has synthesized with the information, it surfaces as well. Your first reaction is, "Let's get away from this ledge!" The second experience created a subsequent synthesizing event.

Once you have left harm's way and are in a safe place, the initial synthesizing event is once again stored in your Subconscious Mind, and the subsequent synthesizing event is stored for the first time. Now you have two subconsciously stored pieces of information (or experiences) to support your fear of heights, and so on.

I can locate and access the initial synthesizing event relating to any subject using muscle testing because your physical body has stored and remembered every experience you have ever had. All the good ones, and all the bad ones.

Imagine an onion. Its center represents the kind of player you would like to become. Over the years you have accumulated layers of synthesizing events. These synthesizing events are responsible for creating the problems you are now experiencing with your athletic performance, and if you don't get rid of it you will carry it with you from game to game. In order to access the center of your onion (your true potential), the layers of synthesizing events must be peeled away, and that is exactly what HK and this program will help you do.

It is my belief that 95% of all synthesizing events are stored in your Subconscious Mind during a period in your childhood development known as the Egocentric Stage.

The Egocentric Stage

There is a period in our childhood known as the "egocentric stage," and it occurs between conception and 7 to 8 years of age. It is during this stage in our development when most of the synthesizing events were stored in your Subconscious Mind.

Webster's defines egocentricity as, "Regarding the self or the individual as the center of all things; Having little or no regard for interests or feelings other than one's own; Self-centered." The egocentric child is so self-centered that the first thought they have when something goes wrong in their lives is, "What did I do wrong?"

If you ask a three-year-old boy if he has a brother, he will answer yes. If you ask that same three-year-old boy if his brother has a brother, he will answer no. That's because the egocentric child cannot objectify his experience, he can only experience. The reason for this phenomenon is that the egocentric child's Mind does not possess a critical factor.

Remember that the critical factor allows your Mind to accept or reject incoming information passing through your Conscious Mind. Without the capacity to criticize incoming information, the egocentric child's Subconscious Mind stores everything! At age 7 or 8 the child's critical factor starts kicking in. During the child's teen years, it is operating at full capacity because teenagers know everything and adults know nothing.

After the teen years, our criticalness starts reversing and by middle age, most of us experience a softening of our attitudes and come to realize that criticism was all a waste of good energy to begin with.

The absence of the critical factor also denies the egocentric child the capacity to rationalize. You cannot rationalize with someone who is incapable of objectifying his experiences. Some of the other anomalies associated with the egocentric child:

* Absolutize – You either love me or you hate me;
* Personalize - Takes everything personally;
* Idealize their role models – If dad says I'm stupid, it must be true;
* Self-blame – What did I do wrong;
* Shame – There must be something wrong with me;

Children have very limited resources when dealing with trauma. The only way they know how to deal with trauma is to block it out. They accomplish this by switching off one or both hemispheres of their brains depending on the severity of the trauma. This switching off will influence the decisions they make for the rest of their lives.

In the 1980's John Bradshaw brought to light much information relating to dysfunctional families. In a dysfunctional family, the members are simply not getting their needs met. What kinds of needs? The need to be loved, nurtured and respected.

So, what kind of a family environment would produce a functional child or adult? The following quote is from a book titled Trauma and Recovery by Dr. Judith Herman:

"The developing child's positive sense of self depends upon a caretaker's benign use of power. When a parent, who is so much more powerful than a child, nevertheless shows some regard for that child's individuality and dignity, that child feels valued and respected; he develops self-esteem. He also develops autonomy, that is, a sense of his own separateness within a relationship. He learns to control and regulate his own bodily functions and to form and express his own point of view."

Wouldn't it have been nice to have been raised in this environment? The truth is that 99% of all families are dysfunctional. This dysfunction leaves most children who experience it filled with shame and doubt. Dr. Herman continues:

"Shame is a response to helplessness, the violation of bodily integrity, and the indignity suffered in the eyes of another person. Doubt reflects the inability to maintain one's own separate point of view while remaining in connection with others. In the aftermath of traumatic events, survivors doubt both others and themselves."

If you show a child respect he will learn to

respect himself and others. Disrespecting a child traumatizes the child and creates a synthesizing event. The switching off anomaly doesn't make children who experience it functional. Relatively speaking, it makes them more functional. They become functional at the expense of some other anomaly they create to compensate.

Also, it is during this stage in our development that we accepted beliefs about ourselves that simply were not true. We accepted beliefs that we were not tall enough, thin enough, smart enough, this enough or that enough.

If you have ever accepted a belief about yourself that you weren't good enough during this stage of your development IT WASN'T TRUE! Please know you accepted that belief during a time in your development when you did not possess a Critical Factor and you were incapable of objectifying and rejecting that information or belief.

Here is an extraordinary example of how things we learn about ourselves during the egocentric stage of our development stay with us the rest of our lives. One day a teacher asked her students to list the names of the other students in the room on two sheets of paper, leaving a space between each name. Then she told them to think of the nicest thing they could say about each of their classmates and write it down. It took the remainder of the class period to finish their assignment, and as the students left the room, each one handed in the papers.

That Saturday, the teacher wrote down the name of each student on a separate sheet of paper, and listed what everyone else had said about that individual. On Monday she gave each student his or her list. Before long, the entire class was smiling. 'Really?' she heard whispered. "I never knew that I meant anything to anyone!" and, "I didn't know others liked me so much," were most of the comments.

No one ever mentioned those papers in class again. She never knew if the students discussed them after class or with their parents, but it didn't matter. The exercise had accomplished its purpose. The students were happy with themselves and one another. That group of students moved on.

Several years later, one of the students was killed in Viet Nam and his teacher attended the funeral of that special student. She had never seen a serviceman in a military coffin before. He looked so handsome, so mature. The church was packed with his friends. One by one those who loved him took a last walk by the coffin. The teacher was the last one to bless the coffin.

As she stood there, one of the soldiers who acted as pallbearer came up to her. "Were you Mark's math teacher?" he asked. She nodded, "Yes." Then he said, "Mark talked about you a lot." After the funeral, most of Mark's former classmates went together to a luncheon. Mark's mother and father were there, obviously waiting to speak with his teacher. "We want to show you something," his father said, taking a wallet out of his pocket. "They found this on Mark when he was killed. We thought you might recognize it."

Opening the billfold, he carefully removed two worn pieces of notebook paper that had obviously been taped, folded and refolded many times. The teacher knew without looking that the papers were the ones on which she had listed all the good things each of Mark's classmates had said about him. 'Thank you so much for doing that," Mark's mother said, "'As you can see, Mark treasured it."

All of Mark's former classmates started to gather around. Charlie smiled rather sheepishly and said, "I still have my list. It's in the top drawer of my desk at home." Chuck's wife said, "Chuck asked me to put his in our wedding album." "I have mine too," Marilyn said, "It's in my diary." Then Vicki, another classmate, reached into her pocketbook, took out her wallet and showed her worn and frazzled list to the group. "I carry this with me at all times," Vicki said and without batting an eyelash, she continued, "I think we all saved our lists."

If you tell a 6 year old he isn't good enough, he has no way of stopping that information. It goes right into subconscious storage and will be used at some point in his future to create his self-image. If you treat that same 6 years with respect and tell him he is loved and cherished he will, likewise, store the information subconsciously and it will have a profound positive impact on his self-image, and he will carry it with him for the rest of his life.

Many children start their football careers playing pee wee football during the egocentric stage of their development. If you are a coach, please be ever mindful of what to tell these children whenever you interact with them. Because they respect you, the will believe everything you tell them.

Sometimes the trauma is so severe that it causes both hemispheres of your brain to weaken or switch off. This creates a condition known as Dissociation.

Dissociation

As I had mentioned earlier, children do not have a lot of options when dealing with trauma. Children deal with it by blocking it out. They accomplish this by switching off one of both hemispheres of their brains depending upon the severity of the trauma. When both hemispheres of the brain switch off it creates a condition known as "dissociation."

Dissociation occurs when specific mental functions become separated (or dissociated) from the mainstream of consciousness and, as a consequence, are lost to the individual's awareness and voluntary control.

When a wide receiver, for instance, dissociates during a pass play he may drop a pass thrown right into his hands. That's becasue he cannot feel (Right Hemisphere switched off), nor is there structure to his physical movement or his mental processes (Left Hemisphere switched off).

Years ago I did a session with a player and asked him to imagine himself making all pro. When I muscle tested, and checked the hemispheres of his brain, they were both switched off. He was experiencing dissociation, and with both hemisperes switched off it's as if the player's body doesn't have access to information provided by the brain. In this mental state the player will never realize his goal. The following year he made all pro.

There is a way to help players keep both hemispheres of their brains switched on during competition and it involves achieving Critical Factor Bypass. This is accomplished with the use of the "HK Performance Trigger."

The HK Performance Trigger

We now know that when an athlete experiences a traumatic encounter, the emotions from that trauma will synthesize with the information stored in his Subconscious Mind and adversely affect his future performances. In order to clear the synthesizing event, a desynthesis must occur. In order to reverse this phenomenon, I employ The HK Performance Trigger.

The HK Performance Trigger is used to release the trauma and all associated emotions connected to that trauma from the player's Subconscious Mind manifesting as stress in his physical body. In other words, the intention of the HK Performance Trigger is to sever the emotional trauma from the information stored in the player's Subconscious Mind creating the stress in his physical body. It works because "energy follows intention."

The more you do something the better you get at it. So, the more you use the HK Performance Trigger, the stronger and more effective it becomes. The HK Performance Trigger was designed to help you peel away the subconsciously stored synthesizing events responsible for your performance problems during competition.

The HK Performance Trigger is designed to help you perform to the best of your ability. The second part of this book shows you how to program in the HK Performance Trigger, and how to use the remainder of this discipline so that you may gain the maximum benefit. Let's examine how this switching off phenomenon adversely affects your mechanics.

Football Mechanics

Earlier I had mentioned that when there is stress present in your body, it would cause one or both hemispheres of your brain to weaken or switch off. This switching off not only affects your thought processes during your football games, but also can adversely affect you physically.

When stress is present in your body, your body weakens. It is when your body is in this weakened state that you make a critical mental error at a crucial point in the game. However, this weakening also adversely affects what you do physically. Here's why.

The right hemisphere of your brain controls the left side of your physical body, while the left hemisphere of your brain controls the right side. When your right hemisphere weakens or switches off during a play, it weakens the left side of your physical body. When you attempt to execute the play with a weak left side, it dramatically alters the mechanical dynamics of what you are physically attempting to do.

If you are a quarterback, for instance, and you are about ready to throw a 30 yard pass to one of your receivers with a weak left side, the whole mechanics of your throwing motion well be severely altered. There is no way you can throw with any consistency with your body in this weakened state. This weakened state is so subtle it cannot be seen with the naked eye.

This mechanically altered motion applies to every position on the football field whether you are a running back, linebacker or offensive lineman. You will either fumble the ball, miss a tackle that allows the runner to advance into the secondary or miss a block that gets your quarterback sacked.

How many times have you seen an offensive player run into the end zone untouched, and there isn't a defensive player within five yards. All the players on a football team, at one time, have been shown how to correctly execute the moves and nuances relating to their position. The one thing that separates them performance wise is the 5" space between their ears. HK helps you master that 5" space so you perform your best on game day.

HK is specifically designed to provide you a resource. A resource to help you become as mentally prepared for your games as you can possibly become so that you may use that 5" space between your ears to help you play your best and help your team win the game.

I employ the HK Performance Trigger to help you keep both hemispheres of your brain switched on during competition. What you are about to learn in the following pages will help you remain calm, focused and relaxed during your games and that is when you achieve peak performance. (When you are calm and relaxed your brain functions at maximum capacity.) It will also provide you with mental clarity so that the decisions you make on the field support you in doing your best to help your team win the game. You will be shown step by step:

1. How to program in the HK Performance Trigger;
2. How to use the HK Performance Trigger before, during and after your games;
3. How to use the "Mind Mastery For Football DVD & CD";
4. How to use the HK Performance Trigger during practice;
5. How to conduct post game evaluations so that you don't carry synthesizing events with you into your next game;

Let's first show you how to program in the HK Performance Trigger.

Programming In The HK Performance Trigger

There are three steps to programming in the HK Performance Trigger:

Step #1: Read the following statement aloud:

"I, (state your name), now accept and integrate into my mind and body the HK Trigger which is stating, thinking or hearing the word 'relax' and touching the thumb and index fingers of both hands, to immediately and permanently neutralize and remove all synthesizing events manifesting as stress in every cell, organ and tissue of my physical body, and to 'switch on' the left and right hemispheres of my brain as well as my corpus callosum so that all three components function as one allowing me to always remain in present time, and to activate that part of my mind and body that supports and allows me to experience and be open to receive more wealth, health, happiness, peace, joy, prosperity, safety and security in my life, and all other attributes I may require to help me experience the lifestyle of my choosing, to help me successfully accomplish all my goals, and to improve the quality of my life relating to every statement, thought and action I experience, layers one through infinity, and I will never interfere with the physical manifestation of all my goals, needs and desires, and every time I activate my HK Trigger it will become ten times more powerful, and to allow the HK Performance Trigger to help me always stay calm, focused and relaxed during all my football games, and to help me play my best and help my team win every game in which I play, and to assist me in

becoming the best football player at my position, and to help me clear all blockages preventing me from successfully accomplishing all my football and non-football related goals. This or something better."

Step #2: Say the word "relax" and touch the thumb and index fingers of both hands, then release and open your fingers.

Step #3: Read the statement in Step #1 again. Remember to read it aloud so that you involve as many of your senses as possible. The HK Performance Trigger, which is stating or thinking the word "relax" and touching the thumb and index fingers of both hands, is now programmed into your Subconscious Mind.

The HK Performance Trigger is intended to help you stay calm, relaxed and focused during your football games, and most importantly during the mechanical execution of the movements related to your position.

When you can remain relaxed during your football games, both hemispheres of your brain will function at maximum capacity. Since the brain controls all movement in the physical body, this helps keep both sides of your body strong allowing the proper execution of the movements relating to your position.

 It will also provide you with the mental clarity necessary to help you create a strategy that will support you in playing your best. This ultimately results in you making a dramatic impact on the outcome of the game. and helps you contribute to your team's efforts to win the game. Your position play will become more consistent and effective allowing you to perform to the best of your ability.

The HK Performance Trigger was designed to help you:

1. To instantly, automatically and permanently release all trauma from your mind manifesting as stress in your physical body;

2. To instantly, automatically and permanently switch on and strengthen both hemispheres of your brain relating to every statement, thought or action you experience no matter what the activity;

3. To neutralize all initial and subsequent synthesizing events preventing you from playing your best on game day;

4. To help you stay calm, focused and relaxed during your football games and to help you play your best and help your team win;

5. To clear all blockages preventing you from successfully accomplishing all your goals.

There is an excellent process we use in HK to extract information from your Subconscious Mind. I call it is called HK Journaling.

HK Journaling

One of the limitations of the Conscious Mind is that it can only focus on one thing at a time. If you are having problems with your performances during football games, there is usually more than one thing responsible for those problems. The HK Journaling exercise allows you to bring up those problems or the negative experiences you had during your games one at a time in order of their priority.

HK Journaling entails the use of open-ended statements to access subconsciously stored synthesizing events manifesting for you as performance problems during competition. Grab a pencil and a blank piece of paper and draw a line down the center of the page. At the top of the left side of the page write the word Negative. At the top of the right side of the page write the word Positive.

Using open-ended statements list the negative things that occurred for you during your last game on the left side of the page. For instance, let's assume that you are a wide receiver and you have just played a game in which your team lost in overtime. Here is how you would document this information.

1.   One of the negative things that occurred during my game was: I dropped a pass in the end zone that would have won the game for us in regulation;
2.   The second negative thing that occurred during my game was: In the second quarter I ran the wrong pass route which caused an interception;

3 The third negative thing that occurred during my game was: Etc.

After you have finished documenting all the negative things that occurred for you during your football game, go to the top of the right side of the page and document all the positive things that occurred for you.

1.   One of the positive things that occurred during my game was: I had six receptions for 225 yards;
2.   The second positive thing that occurred during my game was: I threw a key block that allowed our running back to score a touchdown in the fourth quarter;
3. The third positive thing that occurred during my game was: Etc.

It is important to also focus on the positive things that occurred during your performance because if you only focus on the negative that is all you will see. It reminds of an old saying I once heard, "You are never as good as you think you are, but you are never as bad either." Looking at both negative and positive elements of your game just gives you a more balanced perspective on what's really going on for you.

As you can clearly see, the HK Journaling exercise allows you to document a tremendous amount of information regarding your performance, and the problems that came up for you during your game. Now, let's discuss how the HK Performance Trigger is used to clear the information that surfaced for you during your post game evaluation.

How To Use The HK Performance Trigger

With the onion analogy I explained that the center of the onion represents the type of player you have the potential to become. What's preventing you from becoming that player are the layers of synthesizing events you have accumulated over the years.

What's creating problems with your athletic performance on the football field right now is the fact that you carry these synthesizing events with you from game to game. It's as if you are walking through a mental revolving door.

I suggest that you do the HK Journaling exercise the evening after each and every game in which you compete. What follows is a four step process that will allow you to peel away the layers of synthesizing events responsible for creating the problems you are now experiencing with your athletic performance during football games:

Step #1: If you haven't already, go back to the chapter on Programming In the HK Performance Trigger. Program in the trigger by following Steps 1 through 3 (Once the trigger is programmed in you never have to do it again);

Step #2: Read your HK Journaling list starting with the negative things that came up for you during your most recent game, and read them one at a time;

Step #3: After reading the first item on the negative side of your list, hit your trigger. Say or mentally state the word "relax" and touch the thumb and index fingers of both your hands, and open them. Move to the second negative thing and do the same thing until you have gone through the entire negative list;

Step #4:   Now, move to the positive list and repeat the procedure until you have gone through the entire positive list;

My suggestion is to punch holes in the completed form and store them in a three ring binder. Once a month or so, review them and see if you can find any reoccurring patterns that may be developing in your football game that may need addressing. In fact, the question you should be asking yourself after each game is, "What could I have done to improve my play during this game?"

If you don't think this process is effective, Byron Nelson, a former PGA Tour player, won 18 tournaments (11 in a row!) in one year back in the 1940's doing the exact same thing. If it worked for him, it will certainly work for you.

The HK Performance Trigger can also be used during practice and in regular games as a Pre-Play Routine.

The Pre-Play Routine

You will be integrating this pre-play routine into your practices and regular football games for one reason and one reason only, to help you become as calm and relaxed as possible during the execution of your plays relating to your position.

When you are calm and relaxed during the execution of your plays, it allows you to keep both hemispheres of your brain switched on so that you are mentally sharp and alert. It also helps to keep both sides of your physical body strong.

This allows you to mechanically execute the movement relative to your position in a way that enables you to make the play. Here's how the pre-play routine can be used in real game situations.

Let's assume you are a defensive lineman and it's 3rd and long, and an obvious passing situation. Here's how you do the pre-play routine during a game:

1. Before the play mentally state your goal (i.e., my goal is to sack the quarterback for a loss);
2. Mentally state the word "relax" and proceed to play the down;

There are many reasons why this pre-play routine is so effective. The most important reason is that it allows you to remain focused on your whole purpose for being out there, and that is to play your best and help your team win the game. It also allows you to set a goal for each play, and the continued use of the HK Performance Trigger will help you stay calm, relaxed and focused. Remaining relaxed allows for full availability and use of all your mental and physical faculties.

Another excellent advantage in using this pre-point routine is a phenomenon known as "compounding." Compounding occurs when the same suggestion is layered upon itself many times. The incessant use of the word relax will eventually condition your body to relax. Your play will become much more consistent and effective, and you may even begin to enjoy the experience.

Using The Trigger During The Game

The HK Performance Trigger can also be used during the game to do a quick mini evaluation of a particular play or possession series. The intention of this procedure is to prevent you from carrying synthesizing events from one play or possession series to the next.

For example, let's assume that you are a defensive back and the opposing team's wide receiver just caught a 30 yard pass right in front of you that gave them 1st and 10 in your team's red zone. Ask yourself, "Why wasn't I able to break up that play?" Then mentally state the word "relax." This allows you to clear whatever occurred mentally for you that prevented you from breaking up the play.

Here's why. When you asked the question about your missed play, your Conscious Mind sent instructions to your Subconscious Mind, "Send me all the information you have in storage relating to the play I just missed?" When that information comes up into your Conscious Mind, it will bring any synthesizing events associated with it as well. When you hit your HK Performance Trigger, it allows you neutralize and clear away yet another layer of this onion that has grown around your football game.

Remember that it has taken you years to create the many layers of synthesizing events that make up your mental onion, and that you have been carrying these synthesizing events with you from game to game for years. Continued use of the HK Performance Trigger will help to accelerate the removal of these layers responsible for your marginal play during football games and put an end to this vicious cycle. It allows you to "peel the onion" so that you may get to the center which represents your true potential to become a premier player at your position.

Your physical body never does anything arbitrarily. If you miss a play that causes your team to lose an important game, something motivated your body to do that. Doing these mini evaluations and using the HK Performance Trigger helps you remain mentally clear of any psychological anomalies that may have surfaced for you during your game contributing to your marginal performance on the field.

Doing this process prevents you from carrying the subconsciously stored information responsible for your missed play with you into the next play, possession or game.

Mind Mastery For Football

Years ago I produced a DVD called *Change Your Thinking, Change Your Life.* The DVD explains HK and how I use muscle testing when working with individuals to help them clear blockages preventing them from successfully accomplishing their goals. It even shows you how to muscle test yourself.

I also created a powerful 30 minute CD titled *Winning At Football.* The CD is meant to work on a subconscious level. At the beginning of the CD I have programmed in the same HK Performance Trigger (relax) contained in this book. The CD contains over 100 statements relating to football and winning. Each statement is followed by the trigger word "relax."

Listening to the CD before your game helps put you in a mental space that will allow you to play your best during the game. It will give you an excellent pre-game mental preparation regime that will help clear the mental cobwebs so that the decisions you make during the game helps support your team in winning.

Listening to the CD after your game helps to peel away layers of synthesizing events that came up for you during the course of your performance on the field. If you are not playing to the best of your ability, it simply means that your "stuff" came up during your game. This stuff, in the form of synthesizing events, is responsible for the performance problems you experienced during your game.

If you have been playing football for 10 years, you have 10 years of information stored in your Subconscious Mind. If some of that information was contaminated with synthesizing events, it was put there in layers over this 10 year period.

Listening to the CD helps to accelerate the peeling away of these layers of synthesizing events and puts you on the road to becoming the player you would like to become. It literally changes the subconsciously stored information you have accumulated over the years relating to you and football.

These layers of synthesizing events must be removed in layers because that's the way they were stored. Listening to the CD the evening after each game will allow you to clear whatever "stuff" came up for you earlier that day. If you experience a really horrible game that's when you really need to listen to the CD. Please do your best to remain objective.

I recommend that you listen to the *Winning At Football* CD every day for the first 30 days. After 30 days, listen to the CD one to two hours before game time, and the evening after you play or practice. Find a quiet location to sit or recline comfortably.

Do your best to listen to every statement. If you take a deep breath or yawn after hearing a statement it simply means that a subtle energy shift in your Subconscious Mind has occurred relating to one of the statements you heard on the CD.

I suggest that you buy a small portable CD player and place it on the headboard of you bed. Turn it on before you drift off to sleep and hit repeat with the volume very low. Although it is optimal to listen to the CD while in a conscious waking state, you will still derive benefits listening to the CD as you drift off to sleep. You may also listen to the CD in your car on the way to the game, jogging, etc.

I cannot adequately stress the significance of listening to the CD every day you touch a football. Even when you practice you are accessing information from your Subconscious Mind relating to football.

Some of the information you access during your practice sessions will have synthesizing events attached to them as well, and they must be neutralized or you will carry them into your next game. Listening to the CD helps you to accelerate this process.

This is an e-mail I recently received from a player:

"I bought your Mind Mastery For Football program about a month ago. I was a second string wide receiver, hoping to get into the game. Well, after the first two games, I was placed on the 1st offense and I am now a main target on most pass plays. My confidence has grown a great deal. The concept of relaxing

makes a great deal of sense to me and I have a much better understanding of it by being in game situations.

Your Mind Mastery For Football program has really helped me focus and concentrate. Even though our season has not been a winning one, I feel that the use of your program has helped me make a dramatic difference, when otherwise it may have turned out very differently."

A.B.
Massachusetts

Setting Goals

After Tiger Woods won his first Masters, he skipped a tournament, and came back and won the next tournament. During his post tournament interview he was asked why he thought he won the tournament. Tiger Woods looked at the interviewer surprisingly and replied, "Because it was my goal to win it."

How does your physical body know what your mind expects from it if you do not set a goal? Set a goal for each game and play. Even if your body sabotages your efforts when you set a goal, at least give it the benefit of the doubt. ALWAYS SET A GOAL!!!

Here's what you do to set a goal for each game. The night before each game, grab a pencil and paper and write your goal. After writing your goal, read it aloud. Suppose you are a defensive back. Here's how you would set your goal.

Example:

Step #1: I, player's name, now choose to do everything in my power to help my team win our game tomorrow against (opponent). I will accomplish this by remaining calm, focused and relaxed when playing my position, and I will not allow a reception by any receiver on the opposing team in my area of responsibility. I will never lose sight of my goal to help my team win the game, and I will never do anything to interfere with the successful accomplishment of this goal. This or something better. (Modify goal with # of interception; quarterback sacks on blitzes; Etc.)

Step #2: Hit your HK Performance Trigger by stating or thinking the word "relax" and touching the thumb and index fingers of both hands, and opening them;

Step #3: Read your goal aloud again.

Anytime you do something different your body sends up a red flag and says something like, "What a minute, nobody sent me a memo, what are you doing?" If you are not accustomed to setting goals, the first several times you do it your body may ignore or sabotage.

When you set a goal before your game one of two things will happen. You will either accomplish your goal, or you will play the worst game you have played in years. Why? Because when you set a goal that is when your "stuff" comes up. There is a saying, "If you don't know where you are going, you will never get there."

Set goals at the beginning of the year. In fact, if you are a defensive lineman: How may sacks would you like to record for the upcoming year; How many tackles; Would you like to make all pro?, etc. Write your goals down and use this process to clear your blockages. Do your best to remain objective and ALWAYS SET GOALS!

Using Your Imagination During Practice

Imagination is defined as, "The action or faculty of forming mental images or concepts of what is not actually present to the senses." When you imagine yourself doing something, you are going to subconsciously access the same information as if you were physically doing it. Using your imagination during your practice sessions has a twofold benefit.

First, since your imagination is located in the right hemisphere of your brain, every time you use it you are exercising that part of your brain. If you can keep the right hemisphere of your brain switched on during practice, you will keep it switched on during your games.

Secondly, your Subconscious Mind cannot distinguish between something real or imagined. Using imagination in conjunction with the HK Performance Trigger allows you to neutralize any synthesizing events you may have stored subconsciously relating to a particular game situation.

Think of the most stressful situation you normally encounter during a normal football game, and mentally imagine yourself in that situation during practice. For instance, if you are a defensive lineman involved in a scrimmage, and your team is going to play the Washington Redskins next Sunday, imagine that the guy on the other side of the line plays for the Redskins and see if you can sack the quarterback during that play.

Before the play, set a goal to sack the quarterback then mentally state the work "relax" and proceed with the play. If you weren't able to do it, ask yourself, "Why wasn't I able to sack the quarterback during that last play?" Then hit your HK Performance Trigger by mentally stating or thinking the word "relax."

The reason this is so effective is because when you make the statement "Why wasn't I able to sack the quarterback during that last play," your Conscious Mind will send instructions to your Subconscious Mind, "Send me all the information you have stored relating to why I wasn't able to sack the quarterback on that last play."

The information that surfaces will no doubt have a synthesizing event attached to it, and hitting your HK Performance Trigger will help you peel yet another layer of this mental onion that has grown around your athletic performances.

When you line up against the Redskins line next week your Subconscious Mind will say, "This looks really familiar," because it cannot distinguish between something real or imagined.

Imagination is so effective that during the final round of the 1994 United States Women's Open Golf Championships, Lauri Merten was on the practice putting green imagining herself putting to win the tournament. Four hours later she was hoisting the trophy as the 1994 United

States Women's Golf Open champion. Imagination is a very powerful and effective tool, and it works. I entreat you to religiously integrate it into your practice regime.

Conclusion

Two weeks before the start of the 1994 NFL preseason, using the techniques outlined in this book, I did an HK session with Eric Swann. He was a first round draft pick two years earlier for the then Phoenix Cardinals and hadn't really done much to distinguish himself as a defensive lineman. I had him state his most important goal which was to become all pro in the upcoming season.

After stating the goal I muscle tested him and he muscle tested weak. Now, here is a player that could bench-press 425 pounds and he muscle tested weak for his goal to make all pro. The statement created so much stress in his physical body that it caused it to weaken. With his body in this weakened state he didn't stand a chance of successfully completing his goal.

I programmed in the HK Performance Trigger, and had him hit his trigger and asked him to restate his goal and muscle tested again. He muscle tested strong. I checked his hemispheres and they were both strong or switched on. We worked on a few more goals and ended the session. How did he do?

Well, the first game he played in after our session was a preseason game against the Chicago Bears. During that game he recorded four quarterback sacks. He went on later that season to make all pro at his position. Two years later he signed a five year $25,000,000.00 contract with a $7,000,000.00 signing bonus.

If you follow the program as outlined in this book you will realize a dramatic improvement to your performance no matter what your position.

I know it is a hard pill for some players to swallow, but it is absolutely imperative that you accept responsibility for the experiences you create on and off the football field. I don't suggest it so that you can beat yourself up for all the struggle you have created with your athletic performance. I suggest it so you can get to the second stage of the change process which is, "If I am creating this experience what can I do to change it?" A funny thing happens when you asked yourself this question. Things start to change.

I personally don't know what you are going to have to do to become a premier football player at your position, but on some level of your awareness you do. That information is stored somewhere in your Subconscious Mind. The stress present in your body during competition is actually blocking you from obtaining access to that information.

Doing this program faithfully, will help peel away those blockages preventing you from becoming a premier player at your position. To gain the maximum benefit from *Mastering The Mental Side Of Football* it is important to use the entire program which entails:

- Programming in the HK Performance Trigger;

- Using your HK Performance Trigger along with your imagination during practice;
- Setting goals before each season, game and play;
- Performing mini evaluations while you are on the bench between series and using your HK Performance Trigger;
- Faithfully doing your post tournament evaluations using the HK Journaling exercise;
- Religiously listening to the CD *Winning At Football* before and after your games.

It is said that adversity introduces a man to himself. I trust that the next time you encounter adversity on the football field that you will remain objective enough to understand where it came from and how to constructively deal with it.

Someone wrote years ago, "We can't be Batman to all the Robins in the world." You cannot control what other people think about you, but you can control what you thinks about you. And, believe you me, that is a full time job. The only person you have the control to change is you! Please remember, football, like life, is relative, and that among the blind, the one eyed man is King. "Relax"

***

HK Mind Mastery programs (DVD& CD):

Mind Mastery For Golf
Mind Mastery For Soccer
Mind Mastery For Tennis
Mind Mastery For Hitting
Mind Mastery For Pitching
Mind Mastery For Coaching
Mind Mastery For Basketball
Mind Mastery For Winning
Mind Mastery For Money
Mind Mastery For Selling
Mind Mastery For Peace of Mind
Mind Mastery For Learning
Mind Mastery For Weight Loss
Change Your Thinking Change Your Life (DVD)

Other books by Ernest Solivan:

Quantum Psychophysics (A Treatise on HK)
Mastering The Mental Side of Soccer
Mastering The Mental Side of Tennis
Mastering The Mental Side of Hitting
Mastering The Mental Side of Football
Mastering The Mental Side of Pitching
Mastering The Mental Side of Coaching
Mastering The Mental Side of Basketball
Mastering The Mental Side of Winning
Mastering The Mental Side of Putting
Mastering The Mental Side of Tournament Golf
Pro Se Cites & Authorities

For more information about HK contact:

Performance Consultants International
Website: www.hk-relax.com

www.ingramcontent.com/pod-product-compliance
Lightning Source LLC
Chambersburg PA
CBHW021341090426
42742CB00008B/691